*E*verglades National Park is a subtropic environment that reveals its secrets slowly to those who explore its diversity of plant and animal life. The sky, the sun, summer storms, the shapes and forms of light and shadow play over this savanna-like landscape that birds, plants, insects, fish, and a dozen endangered species call home.

N ative Americans discovered it first. A Renaissance woman, Marjory Stoneman Douglas, made it known. In historic time "Pa-hay-okee" or "the grassy waters" could be canoed for endless miles. The Shark River Slough, not much more than a few feet deep, is the lifeblood of the Everglades.

Everglades National Park, *in south Florida, was established in 1947 to preserve the unique flora and fauna of the Everglades.*

Front cover: Male anhinga, photo by Glenn Van Nimwegen. Inside front cover: Dwarf cypress, photo by David Muench. Page 1: Evening flight of white ibis, photo by Glenn Van Nimwegen. Pages 2/3: Paddling through the Shark River Slough, photo by Fred Hirschmann. Pages 4/5: Early morning ranger-led bird walk on the Anhinga trail, photo by Glenn Van Nimwegen.

Edited by Cheri C. Madison.
Book design by K. C. DenDooven.

Fourth Printing, 1998

in pictures EVERGLADES The Continuing Story
© 1989 KC PUBLICATIONS, INC.

*"The Story Behind the Scenery"; "in pictures... The Continuing Story";
the parallelogram forms and colors within are registered
in the U.S. Patent and Trademark Office.*

LC 89-80844. ISBN 0-88714-040-8.

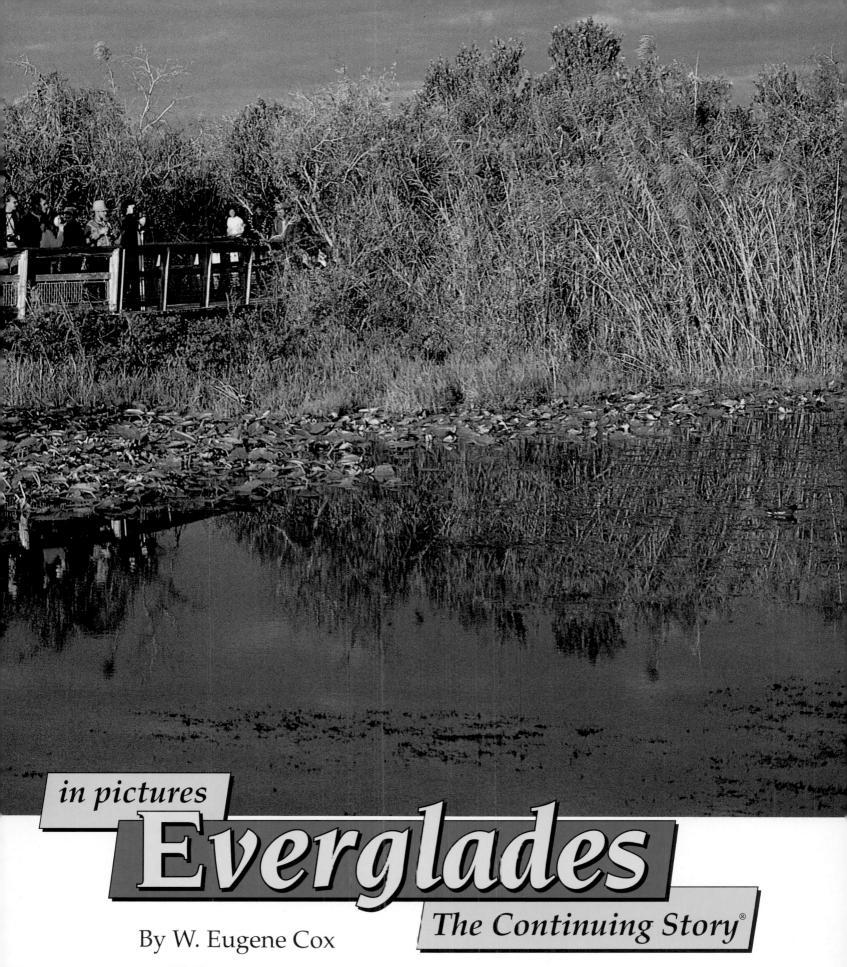

in pictures

Everglades

The Continuing Story®

By W. Eugene Cox

W. Eugene Cox, a graduate of Lincoln Memorial University, is a career employee with the National Park Service and served three years at Everglades. Gene's goal has always been to provide the best possible experience for visitors to America's national parks.

Special thanks to Peter Allen of the National Park Service for revising this updated version.

National park areas are special landscapes set aside by acts of Congress to protect and preserve features of national significance that are generally categorized as scenic, scientific, historical, and recreational.

As Americans, we are joint caretakers of these unique places, and we gladly share them with visitors from around the world.

Everglades, with its 1,500,000 acres, is the third largest national park in the lower 48 United States. This wilderness has its own special beauty no matter what the weather, which can quickly change from sunshine in the morning to rain in the afternoon. Because of its fragile ecosystem and unique environmental qualities, the United Nations designated this park a Biosphere Reserve in 1976 and in 1979 designated it a World Heritage Site. The ecosystem is completely dependent on water flow, and life-giving summer thunderstorms complete the natural cycle. Unlike many places, the line here between survival and death can be measured in a few inches of water.

CONNIE TOOPS

Tropical rainstorms replenish the glades and provide for a rich diversity of life in the park.

The Blending of Land and Sea

Everglades National Park is part of the larger south Florida ecosystem consisting of about 8,000,000 acres that is known as the Everglades. Imagine it as a land slightly tilted toward the sea forming the southern peninsula of Florida. A tilt so gradual in elevation that before south Florida was settled, a large shallow river many miles wide flowed uninterrupted across this marshland. Never more than a few feet deep and approximately 40 miles wide, it flowed 240 miles to the estuaries of Florida Bay and the Gulf of Mexico. In these wetlands, saw grass (technically a sedge, not a grass) gives way to the coastal mangrove forest where organisms feeding on detritus (decaying materials) eventually become food for game fish such as tarpon and snook.

RUSS FINLEY

△ **Wherever fresh and sea waters meet in** mangrove forests, they provide one of the most significant estuary environments in the world. The root systems of mangroves provide a nursery for many marine animals, and their branches rest stops for migratory birds.

Geologically Florida Bay is ▷ very young. The mud sedimentation above the Miami limestone was deposited about 4,000 years ago and is a process that continues today. Geologists from throughout the world come to find clues to the geological past of similar limestone formations, which may contain oil.

Florida Bay—A Valuable Marine Nursery

△ **Florida Bay, where the freshwater Everglades meets the Gulf of Mexico, is** *unsurpassed in beauty. This shallow coastal water, not much more than six feet deep, with emerald bays and estuaries, is fringed with mangroves. Small mangrove keys, or islands, appear to float like ships upon the horizon. At sunset the ritual passage of hundreds of wading birds may be observed as they seek the refuge of these protected sites. At low tide mud banks are evident, exposing critically important sea grass habitat which provides food and shelter for undersea life. Researchers have documented that this 850-square-mile estuary serves as a nursery for such creatures as spiny lobster, pink shrimp, stone crab, and gray snapper. These species provide over $30 million in income to Florida fisheries each year.*

CARR CLIFTON

CONNIE TOOPS

△ **These mangrove prop** roots appear to be like legs marching into the tidal shallows to hold and build land, which is exactly what they do! The roots cling to the soil and reduce wave action, while at the same time catching and holding silt and detritus to form new ground.

Perhaps a similar view of a ▷ morning glory on Northwest Cape Sable Beach inspired Horace M. Albright, second director of the National Park Service, to say in a 1930 Congressional hearing that "the Cape Sable area is one of the most beautiful places I have ever seen anywhere."

◁ **_The_ transition zone** △
where saw grass and mangrove mingle illustrates the ability of the red mangrove to live in both fresh and brackish water. This red mangrove brightens the cracking mud flats until the waters of summer return. In the spring it blossoms with yellow flowers. Its prop roots help stabilize shorelines against hurricanes. In the freshwater swamp lying above the limestone rock formation of the Everglades, red mangroves seem to seek solution holes (dissolved by acid from decaying vegetation) which provide the anchorage for roots, nutrients, and water needed for growth. It is a struggle to live in this habitat.

GLENN VAN NIMWEGEN

Water— Controller of Life

***T**his tranquil scene of a* ▷ *swamp lily and a dwarf cypress tree belies the dangers facing a park that is perhaps the most ecologically threatened in the nation. Some 1,400 miles of canals and 125 water control structures restrict the historic water flow to the park. The quantity, quality, timing, and distribution of freshwater deliveries are critical to restoring as nearly as possible this historic water flow for plants and wildlife. Reproductive cycles of birds, alligators, and other wildlife depend on natural seasonal water fluctuations. Research has shown that the health of the marine estuary in Florida Bay is also closely connected to freshwater deliveries.*

LEONARD LEE RUE III

GLENN VAN NIMWEGEN

△ ***T**he playful otter is most frequently seen in the Shark Valley area when water levels drop. This fish-eating mammal is one of many animals in the park that rely on an adequate supply of water to maintain their food sources.*

13

Hammocks—A Forest in a Saw Grass Prairie

The skyline reveals the low ▷ silhouette of hammocks in the saw grass prairie. In the United States, the tropical hardwood hammock is found only in Florida and its unique characteristics often intrigue the observer. More than 60 percent of the native species of trees in a hammock are West Indian in origin. Located on slightly elevated land, hammocks are dominated by West Indian hardwood species such as gumbo limbo, bustics, mastics, wild coffee, and the toxic poisonwood.

GLENN VAN NIMWEGEN

GLENN VAN NIMWEGEN

◁ **T**he Boston fern is a graceful terrestrial from the American tropics. A hammock plant, it grows in humus, on trees or where there is exposed limestone. Although commonly found in the shade, the Boston fern's tolerance for sunlight allows it to grow in open, sunny spots. Due to Florida's unique geographical position, both temperate and tropic species abound.

*T*he lovely, intricate, almost lacy ▷
pattern of strangler fig roots has a
death grip on this cypress tree. Years
earlier, a seed was possibly carried by a
bird into the branches of this host tree.
Although not a true parasite, the
strangler fig will spend years growing
on the tree. The downward spiraling
roots will become established in the soil,
eventually engulfing the cypress. Good
examples of this may be found on the
Otter Cave trail at Shark Valley and
along the Mahogany Hammock trail.

GLENN VAN NIMWEGEN

Palms, Pines and Limestone

R.F. HEAD—EARTH SCENES

The Atlantic Coastal ▷
Ridge begins north of Miami and
follows the coast southward,
eventually making a westward
turn into the park. This elevated
ground is habitat for the slash
pine which once covered almost
200,000 acres of this land.
Today, the last remnants in
south Florida, about 20,000
acres, are preserved in the park.

◁ **A**lthough native to
Florida, the threatened
paurotis palm is more
common to the West Indies,
western Cuba, Yucatan, and
Belize. The weather from the
Caribbean has a strong
influence on south Florida's
flora and fauna. Hurricanes
and even strong winds can
carry a variety of plants and
birds to the park.

The park is ▷
underlaid near the surface
with oolite or Miami
limestone dating to about
100,000 years ago.
Known locally as
"pinnacle rock," this
exposed limestone
erodes rapidly, creating
bizarre shapes and sharp
jagged edges that hamper
foot travel in the
Everglades.

GLENN VAN NIMWEGEN

Enjoy—

Our National Parks

*The Culture of
our Native Americans*

*for those who then
want to know more*
We have a complete series of books

THE STORY BEHIND THE SCENERY®

FRED HIRSCHMANN

▲ *The beautiful great egret, one of the most commonly seen birds, was once hunted to near-extinction by late nineteenth and early twentieth century plume hunters.*

Diversity of Life

Everglades National Park is at the end of a vast wetland water system that begins roughly 240 miles to the north in the Kissimmee Basin. This flat terrain drops only an average of two inches per mile. As water flows across the landscape, the slightest variation in water levels can mean the loss of feeding habitat for birds or the flooding of alligator nests. This fragile ecosystem supports more than 350 species of birds and over 1,000 species of plants, including 120 species of trees. The varied environments in the park include marine estuaries, mangrove forests, cypress strands, saw grass, hammocks, and slash pine forest. In these multiple habitats the park provides protection for over a dozen endangered species. More than any other park in the country, Everglades exists at the pleasure of man. Water is the source of life for the park, and human-controlled water deliveries determine whether it will survive or not.

JAMES A. KERN

◀ *The male fiddler crab seems to hold its large claw like a fiddle as it defends its territory. On mud flats this burrowing crab plugs its mudhole to keep out the rising water and lives on the oxygen trapped within.*

CONNIE TOOPS

CONNIE TOOPS

△ *The Pa-hay-okee overlook* is strategically placed where three distinct habitats of the Everglades ecosystem may be observed. The trail is nestled in a hardwood hammock of tropical plants. A nearby observation tower provides views of endless vistas across both a freshwater saw grass prairie and a cypress strand.

◁ *Alligators, once* threatened with extinction, have made an amazing recovery. Called "the caretakers of the glades," they dig holes that provide water for wildlife during the dry season.

The Feathered Spectacle

▲ *The beauty of the Everglades is enhanced by its birds even as the tragedy of the Everglades is* being told by its birds. Will we listen? Unusual birds may be found in the park, especially during winter and during migration when many birds come from the West Indies. The Florida peninsula is popular with wading birds which generally nest in winter and spring. Breeding season is carefully timed to obtain the necessary food. As the water becomes more shallow and pools form which collect fish, birds feed more easily and abundantly. Water level fluctuation can, therefore, determine the success or failure of breeding and nesting. Population loss occurred initially from 30 to 40 years of plume hunting and continues because of habitat destruction and the absence of a natural water flow through the park. Consider this startling fact: The population of nesting wading birds in the park has secreased from 300,000 in the 1930s to 10,000 in the 1990s. Fortunately, steps to reverse this decline are now being taken.

***T**he almost*
*ethereal view of the
snowy egret is a delight
to photographers. This
bird will fly long
distances to feed. Its
active feeding habits are
noticeable when it stirs
the shallow water to
attract fish and aquatic
life by the flash of its
yellow feet. Found in
North and South
America, it favors salt or
brackish water during
the breeding season.*

***O**bserving
roseate spoonbills
in breeding
plumage is truly a
memorable
experience. When
feeding, they
rhythmically swing
their spatulate bills
from side to side.*

21

◁ **T**here are only about 2,000 snail kites left in the United States. This bird was disappearing even before the amended endangered species list was established in 1973. It feeds almost exclusively on apple snails. A specialized feeder, its hooked bill is adapted to extracting the snail from its shell.

IRENE HINKE-SACILOTTO

FRED HIRSCHMANN

△ **The purple gallinule is a striking bird which** has a limited range in the United States. Its large feet help disperse its weight so it can walk across aquatic plants looking for insects.

◁ **There were 12,000 nesting pairs of wood** storks in the south Florida wetlands during the 1930s. By the late 1980s over a 90 percent decline had occurred. This endangered species is referred to as the "barometer of the Everglades." Storks have a long nesting cycle which, unfortunately, starts late in the Everglades due to continued loss of peripheral wetlands and the elimination of early dry season feeding grounds. Massive efforts now underway seek to restore water flow and other natural conditions beneficial to wood storks and other Everglades life.

CONNIE TOOPS

△ **If this largest of the herons is not** preening, then the great blue may be observed as it slowly and regally hunts through the shallows.

Overleaf: For a brief time in dry winters, ▷ hundreds of wading birds congregate as the water level at Mrazek Pond drops. Photo by Glenn Van Nimwegen.

◁ **Found throughout** the southeastern coastal areas of the United States, the yellow-crowned night heron lives in a variety of habitats, usually roosting in trees. Its range extends from New York to the upper coastlines of South America.

▲ **The solitary green-backed** heron is usually more difficult to find along the water's edge.

Color and its habit of diving head ▷ first into the water after its prey distinguish this brown pelican from the white pelican. Both use their huge throat pouches as dip nets to catch their food.

An Unending Variety of Birds

▲ **The American coot was hunted** extensively before the creation of the park. The first privately owned land for the park, located at Coot Bay, was purchased in 1947 from the Shark River Fishing Camp, Inc. This was the site of one of the first ranger stations.

▲ **Frequently seen throughout the marine sections** of the park, the osprey is a common resident of the Ten Thousand Islands.

It takes about five ▷ years for the southern bald eagle to attain its adult plumage. Records indicate eagles have been nesting in the park since at least the mid-1800s. The 52 nesting pairs in the park represent about 15 percent of the total Florida population of this endangered species.

ALAN & SANDY CAREY

LEONARD LEE RUE III

◁ *Everglades is the only place in the world where both alligators and crocodiles* △ *live. Alligators perform a valuable service for themselves and other animals by digging holes that hold water for the dry season. In these "gator holes," fish congregate and provide food for birds as well as alligators. The mixture of plants and soil that the alligator removes during the excavation process provides nutrients for seedlings. Once growth takes place, an aerial view of these tree islands suggests a doughnut with the water being the hole. The alligator's diet consists of fish, snails, turtles, and small mammals. They can even be cannibalistic when the food supply is low. Being cold-blooded, they must soak up the sun's rays in order to function, so they are often seen lounging on the banks or lazily swimming in the water. When agitated they can move very rapidly. True alligators are native only to the United States and China. The Chinese alligator lives in totally developed agricultural areas and is probably near extinction. Efforts are being taken by the Chinese to save this reptile.*

ALAN & SANDY CAREY

An endangered ▷
*species, crocodiles
are related to alligators
but prefer salty or
brackish water. The
park has established a
crocodile sanctuary
in northeast Florida Bay.
There are only about
400 of these secretive
reptiles in Everglades
National Park and
about 100 outside
its boundaries.*

◁ **T**his beautiful endangered tawny cat is an excellent but tragic example of the delicate balance of nature in south Florida. Man's encroachment on its habitat and food sources have almost spelled the end of the Florida panther. There are fewer than 50 left in Florida and less than 10 in Everglades National Park.

ALAN & SANDY CAREY

▽ **A**lthough normally a nocturnal animal, the opossum may sometimes be seen during the day. It has adapted in this semi-watery environment to practically all the different habitats.

ALAN & SANDY CAREY

▽ **O**ne of the most common North American mammals, the raccoon is known for its cunning and curiosity. Raccoons favor the wetlands and the brackish lagoons. Along the coast they prey upon the nests of the loggerhead turtle in early summer.

CONNIE TOOPS

Other Everglades Residents

DALE TAYLOR

IRENE HINKE-SACILOTTO

▲ *The endangered Cape Sable seaside* sparrow, found in Everglades National Park and Big Cypress National Preserve, is unique as it has an inland range.

▲ *The Florida white-tailed deer is unusual* as it lives almost entirely in a wet environment. It is often observed in the evening feeding on one of its favorite foods, the sedge or saw grass.

CONNIE TOOPS

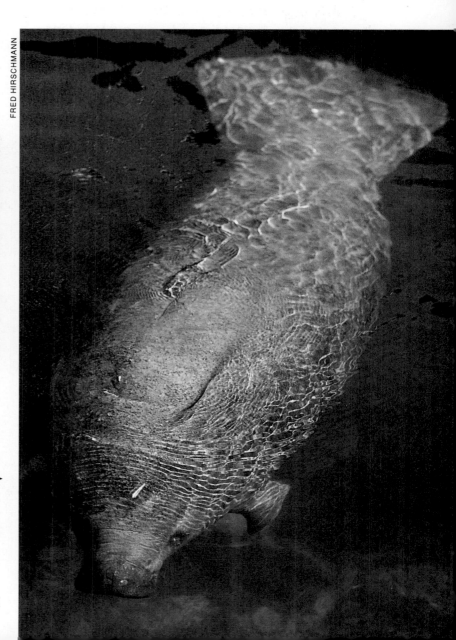

FRED HIRSCHMANN

▲ *A sunfish feeds on animals living on* bladderwort. As water levels drop, the sunfish is the first to perish because of oxygen deprivation.

Florida's state marine mammal, the manatee, ▷ feeds on submerged plants near the water's edge. As many as 200 manatees, 10 percent of their Gulf Coast population, winter in the quiet waters of Everglades National Park.

The Little Things of Life

One small mangrove leaf drops silently into the estuary. An insignificant happening? Perhaps. But when an acre of healthy mangroves shed their leaves, about three tons of leaves accumulate annually. When decomposition occurs, these leaves become part of a complex food chain which feeds shrimp, small fish, wading birds, and eventually people....A winter resident of the West Indies, the white-crowned pigeon nests in the park on mangroves and feeds inland on, among other things, poisonwood berries.

▲ **F**ound usually in freshwater habitats, the green tree frog's breeding call may be heard March through October. Occasionally it may be observed in brackish waters.

◁ **T**he displayed throat fan of the green anole indicates courtship ritual or is used in defense of its territory. The only anole species native to the continental United States, it is most often observed in shrubs, trees, and vines.

The Florida atala ▷
is a threatened butterfly whose larvae feed on a threatened plant. The plant, Florida coontie, grows in tropical hammocks and slash pine forests.

◁ *T*he apple snail is common in the park and is an important △
food source for the snail kite. Apple snails are part of the diet for other birds as well. Snail eggs are laid on emergent vegetation once water levels have risen. During the dry season, the snails burrow in the mud until water and algae return.

△ *T*his walking stick is doing something most
of us cannot do: touching the poisonwood leaves without getting blisters.

△ *L*ike many of the species of the
Everglades, the yellow and black argiope spider lives in both tropic and temperate regions. It is an orb weaver and normally has these zigzag patterns in its web. Vibration and tension in the web signal a captive.

An Abundance of Plants

*T*he box briar is a shrub ▷
native to south Florida.

CONNIE TOOPS

CONNIE TOOPS

M.P. KAHL—DRK PHOTO

▲ *Orchids and bromeliads, which* have migrated from the tropics, are the most numerous epiphytes, or "air plants," found in the park.

◁ *T*he lovely pine-pink orchid grows in pinelands or wetlands above the high water level.

GLENN VAN NIMWEGEN

CONNIE TOOPS

▲ *T*he nicker bean grows along the coast.

*W*hile exploring Cape Sable in ▷ 1916, botanist John K. Small mentioned "thickets of vicious plants" which were probably yucca, a member of the lily family.

34

△ *The shield fern can be found* in hammocks.

Taylor Slough is the second largest ▷ slough (pronounced "slew") in the park. Its water flow has been disrupted by completion of the L-31W canal at the park boundary. Royal Palm Hammock, adjacent to the slough, has the most diverse habitat of all the park's hammocks. In 1916 a botanical survey reported finding 241 plant species in only 960 acres. This tropical hardwood hammock and the nearby Anhinga trail are the most visited areas in the park. Both are excellent for observing plant and animal life.

◁ *Spatterdock,* or yellow pond lily, is found in slow-moving waters. This native plant hosts the common bonnet worm, which bluegill fish prefer.

▲ *It is unlikely anyone could get very far in a buggy in the vast Everglades. This gentleman probably pulled off one of the few trails to pose for this photograph in 1906.*

Everglades' Early History

When the Spaniards arrived in the 1500s, they found Calusa Indians living along the coast. These Indians had such a bountiful supply of fish and turtles that they were not an agricultural society. Among their legacy are huge shell mounds, such as Chokoloskee in the Ten Thousand Islands. By the 1850s the Seminole wars suggested a need for the white man to explore the largely unmapped interior. Military explorers were among the first to suggest draining the Everglades for farming. Many settlers who came here sought the isolation of the Florida frontier at the turn of the century. A few farmed, most fished commercially, but hunting for fur and feathers was apparently the preferred activity. By the 1920s roads were being built. Man was beginning to change the Everglades forever through his building, draining, and channeling activities.

▲ *In the 1920s efforts were intensified to establish an Everglades National Park. Ernest F. Coe, one of the most ardent supporters, campaigned tirelessly for the park idea. His efforts were so successful he has been called the "father of the Everglades National Park."*

▲ *The Florida Federation of Women's Clubs acquired the Royal Palm Hammock in 1916 to* *preserve its plants and magnificent royal palms. Their efforts and donation of the land to the park were* *recognized by Daniel Beard, first park superintendent, in an October 1947 ceremony.*

▲ *President Harry S Truman proudly accepts,* *from William McKinley Osceola, a finely crafted shirt* *and a purse for Mrs. Truman at the dedication of the* *park on December 6, 1947.*

Between November 1934 and June 1935, ▷ *Civilian Conservation Corps workers built trails* *and a shelter, as well as planting* *541 royal palms in the park.*

People at Everglades

From throughout the world people come to study the biological and ecological diversity in the Everglades. Many visit for the scenic beauty and recreational opportunities. The park is well suited for such visitation, with a variety of interpretive programs and facilities. Educational activities presented by park rangers inform visitors about the distinct habitats and how they all are dependent upon water. Observation towers, boardwalks, and trails with descriptive signs offer close-up views of the flora and fauna. Concession-operated boat tours explore the important coastal mangrove environment. For the adventuresome, the 99 mile wilderness waterway canoe trail is a once-in-a-lifetime trip.

LEONARD LEE RUE III

The red-shouldered hawk is particularly common at Eco Pond in Flamingo, where they breed, hunt, and perch close to visitors.

Early morning fog lifts ▷ gently from the water along the Anhinga trail. A favorite spot for wildlife, it is, naturally, a preferred place for park visitors. Even the intent photographer can become the subject for another. Come join us!

GLENN VAN NIMWEGEN

△ *Visitors investigate firsthand the critically important ecosystem of the Shark River Slough. This river of grass may also be called the river of life. Without water, the delicate balance will be irrevocably changed.*

▽ *As dawn breaks over the Shark Valley observation tower, wildlife activity begins. Nowhere else in the park are visitors on land able to see such a limitless stretch of saw grass prairie. However, only a small percentage of the entire Everglades ecosystem is visible.*

◁ **Visitors explore** the saw grass prairie and learn about the algal mat called periphyton. During the dry season this mat protects about 100 different organisms that will repopulate the Everglades when water returns.

△ **In January photographers** line the banks of Mrazek Pond. When water levels are down and a feeding frenzy is taking place, this is one of the best birding spots in the park.

In this popular ranger ▷ program, visitors are dipnetting for seahorses, hermit crabs, and other marine life. Those netted are returned to the bay.

Seminoles and Miccosukees

The Miccosukee Tribe once belonged to the Creek Indian Nation, as did the Seminoles. Despite their similarities, both tribes have their own histories and traditions. After the last Seminole War (1855-1858), the Miccosukee took refuge in the Everglades. A stable lifestyle was developed through subsistence farming and hunting. By the 1930s drainage canals were dug by the state-managed Everglades Drainage District, reducing game and fish. This disruption forced many from their traditional campsites. Eventually several family groups resettled along the then-newly-constructed Tamiami Trail (U.S. Highway 41). In 1962 the Miccosukee Tribe formally organized itself with about 450 members.

Prior to the ▷ availability of sewing machines at the turn of the century, it took a month to hand sew an intricately designed shirt. Beads, wood carvings, patchwork, and basket weaving are a few of the crafts featured at the Miccosukee Culture Center and Indian Village near Shark Valley.

NPS PHOTO

Restoring the Everglades

Nesting wading birds have declined some 90 percent in the past 60 years. Estuarine areas like Florida and Whitewater bays, so vital to pink shrimp, game fish, lobsters, and blue crabs, have also diminished in productivity. The world's largest water-management system successfully controls flooding throughout south Florida. Unfortunately, this project has also dewatered Everglades National Park. Nearly a billion gallons of water that once nourished the Everglades now wash each year through canals out into the Atlantic Ocean. An enormous effort is underway to change water distribution throughout south Florida. A sprawling canal system is being re-engineered to deliver more natural water flows to Everglades National Park and other south Florida wetlands. The long-term goal of this cooperative effort is to restore the ecological health of the Everglades, while still maintaining flood protection and water supply for the people of south Florida.

NPS PHOTO

Only one year after this area was scraped down to rock, native plants repopulated it. Schools of small fish now feed on native insects and plants within a wetland of saw grass and other species. ▽

NPS PHOTO

Everglades ▷ supports the largest field research program in the National Park Service. Its many research studies are focused on developing the knowledge necessary to guide restoration efforts for the entire ecosystem. Here scientists examine and replace eggs from an alligator nest. Like all Everglades life, the alligator is tied to water management in south Florida.

MARTY CORDANO–DRK PHOTO

△ **S**mall-scale restoration of former farmlands within Everglades National Park requires extreme measures. Dense stands of invasive, non-native Brazilian pepper had taken over this region of disturbed soil. To allow growth of native plant communities, heavy equipment removed all vegetation and soil down to bedrock.

Two release structures, now under construction, will improve water deliveries into the central flowway of Everglades National Park, the Shark River Slough. The four present structures on U.S. Highway 41 provide water release from upstream storage reservoir Conservation Area 3A into the slough. However, these gateways have proven inadequate for ◁▽ maintaining surface water flows into the park.

JAMES A. KERN

GLENN VAN NIMWEGEN

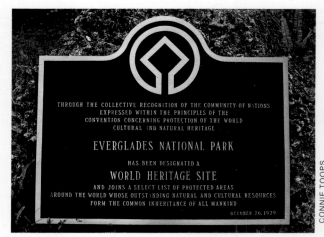

CONNIE TOOPS

△ *Everglades is one of the best outdoor* laboratories for learning more about how to preserve threatened resources. The park is one of only eight areas in the world recognized as both a World Heritage Site and an International Biosphere Reserve.

◁ *Naturally occurring fire is beneficial to the* ecosystem of the park. Natural fires are caused by lightning, and most occur in late spring and early summer. During the wet season, fires are less destructive and more helpful. In slash pine forests, fire retards the saw palmetto understory so that pine regeneration may take place. It also keeps the hardwood trees out of the pine lands. Everglades was the first park to implement prescribed burning in order to maintain a natural mosaic of habitat.

Florida National Parks and Monuments Association, Inc.

Florida National Parks and Monuments Association, Inc. is a private, non-profit organization. Proceeds from sales assist in supporting the educational, scientific, historical and interpretive services of Everglades National Park, Biscayne National Park, Fort Jefferson National Monument, Big Cypress National Preserve, and other activities within the National Park Service.

SUGGESTED READING

CARR, ARCHIE. *The Everglades: The American Wilderness.* New York: Time-Life Books, 1972.

de GOLIA, JACK. *Everglades: The Story Behind the Scenery.* Las Vegas, Nevada: KC Publications, Inc., 1978.

DOUGLAS, MARJORY STONEMAN. *The Everglades: River of Grass.* St. Simons Islands, Georgia: Mockingbird Press, 1947.

GEORGE, JEAN CRAIGHEAD. *Everglades Wildguide.* Washington, D.C.: National Park Service/Govt. Printing Office, 1972, reissued 1987.

ROBERTSON, WILLIAM B., Jr. *Everglades—The Park Story.* Miami: Florida National Parks and Monuments Association, Inc., 1989.

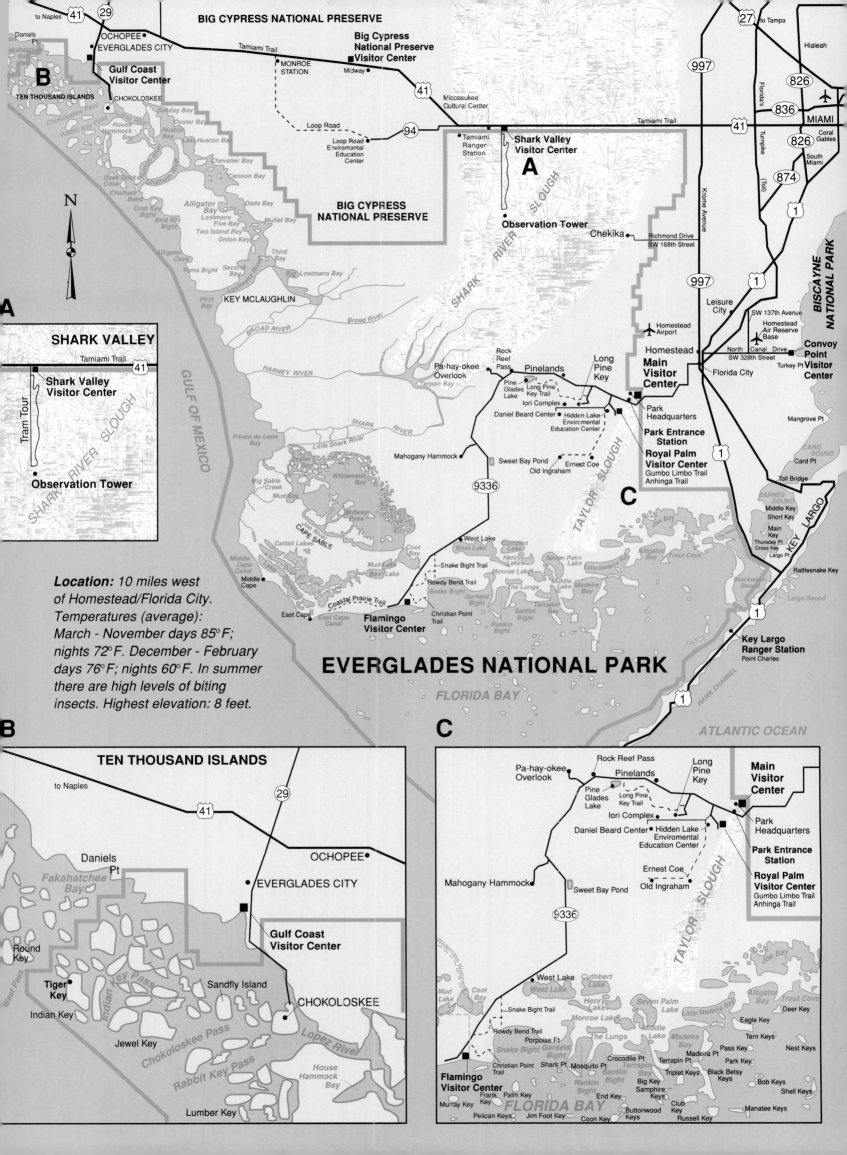

EVERGLADES NATIONAL PARK

BIG CYPRESS NATIONAL PRESERVE

to Naples 41 29
to Tampa 27

OCHOPEE
EVERGLADES CITY
Tamiami Trail
MONROE STATION
Midway
Big Cypress National Preserve Visitor Center
41

B TEN THOUSAND ISLANDS
Gulf Coast Visitor Center
CHOKOLOSKEE

Daniels Pt
Fakahatchee Bay

Loop Road
94
Loop Road Enviromental Education Center

Miccosukee Cultural Center
Tamiami Trail 41 MIAMI
826
836
Hialeah
997

Tamiami Ranger Station
Shark Valley Visitor Center
A

Coral Gables
South Miami
874
826
1

Observation Tower
Chekika
Richmond Drive
SW 168th Street

BIG CYPRESS NATIONAL PRESERVE

Chevelier Bay
Cannon Bay

Leisure City
SW 137th Avenue
997
Homestead Air Reserve Base
North Canal Drive
SW 328th Street

BISCAYNE NATIONAL PARK

Sunday Bay
Oyster Bay
Last Huston Bay
House Hammock Bay

Alligator Bay
Lostmans Five Bay
Two Island Bay
Onion Key
Dads Bay
Mullet Bay

Homestead Airport
Homestead
Main Visitor Center
Florida City

Convoy Point Visitor Center
Turkey Pt
Mangrove Pt

N

Alligator Cove
Toms Bight
Second Bay
Third Bay
Big Lostmans Bay

KEY MCLAUGHLIN

First Bay

Rock Reef Pass
Pa-hay-okee Overlook
Pinelands
Pine Glades Lake
Long Pine Key Trail
Iori Complex
Daniel Beard Center
Hidden Lake Enviromental Education Center

Long Pine Key
Park Headquarters
Park Entrance Station
Royal Palm Visitor Center
Gumbo Limbo Trail
Anhinga Trail

Card Pt
CARD SOUND
Card Pt
Toll Bridge

BROAD RIVER
Broad River

HARNEY RIVER

SHARK RIVER

Tarpon Bay

GULF OF MEXICO

Ponce de Leon Bay

Mahogany Hammock
Sweet Bay Pond
Old Ingraham
Ernest Coe

9336

C

BARNES SOUND
Middle Key
Short Key
Main Key
Thursday Pt
Cross Key
Largo Pt

Little Shark River
Oyster Bay
Whitewater Bay
Mud Bay
Big Sable Creek

Midway Pass
Joe River
CAPE SABLE
Cattail Lakes

Joe Bay
TAYLOR SLOUGH

Blackwater Sound
Largo Sound

Rattlesnake Key

West Lake
Cuthbert Lake
West Lake
Henry Lake
Seven Palm Lakes
Little Madeira Bay
Alligator Bay
Trout Cove

Middle Cape Canal
Lake Ingraham
Mud Lake
Bear Lake
Snake Bight Trail
Monroe Lake
The Lungs
Middle Lake
Madeira Bay

Middle Cape

Rowdy Bend Trail
Snake Bight
Garfield Bight
Terrapin Bay
Santini Bight

East Cape
East Cape Canal
Coastal Prairie Trail
Christian Point Trail
Flamingo Visitor Center
Rankin Bight

Key Largo Ranger Station
Point Charles

Location: 10 miles west of Homestead/Florida City. Temperatures (average): March - November days 85° F; nights 72° F. December - February days 76° F; nights 60° F. In summer there are high levels of biting insects. Highest elevation: 8 feet.

EVERGLADES NATIONAL PARK

FLORIDA BAY

ATLANTIC OCEAN

A

SHARK VALLEY

Tamiami Trail 41
Shark Valley Visitor Center
Tram Tour
Observation Tower
SHARK RIVER SLOUGH

B

TEN THOUSAND ISLANDS

to Naples
41 29
Daniels Pt
Fakahatchee Bay
OCHOPEE
EVERGLADES CITY
Gulf Coast Visitor Center
Round Key
Tiger Key
Indian Key
Sandfly Island
CHOKOLOSKEE
Jewel Key
Chokoloskee Pass
House Hammock Bay
Lopez River
Rabbit Key Pass
West Pass
Indian Key Pass
Lumber Key

C

Rock Reef Pass
Pa-hay-okee Overlook
Pinelands
Pine Glades Lake
Long Pine Key Trail
Long Pine Key
Iori Complex
Daniel Beard Center
Hidden Lake Enviromental Education Center
Main Visitor Center
Park Headquarters
Park Entrance Station
Royal Palm Visitor Center
Gumbo Limbo Trail
Anhinga Trail

Mahogany Hammock
Sweet Bay Pond
Ernest Coe
Old Ingraham
9336

Wilderness Waterway
TAYLOR SLOUGH

West Lake
Cuthbert Lake
West Lake
Coot Bay
Mud Lake
Snake Bight Trail
Henry Lake
Monroe Lake
Seven Palm Lake
Little Madeira Bay
Alligator Bay
Trout Cove

Rowdy Bend Trail
Porpoise Pt
Snake Bight
Garfield Bight
The Lungs
Middle Lake
Madeira Bay

Deer Key
Eagle Key
Tern Keys

Christian Point Trail
Flamingo Visitor Center
Shark Pt
Crocodile Pt
Mosquito Pt
Santini Bight
Terrapin Pt
Terrapin Bay
Madeira Pt
Pass Key
Park Key
Nest Keys

Frank Key
Murray Key
Palm Key
Pelican Keys
Jim Foot Key
Coon Key
End Key
Big Key
Samphire Keys
Triplet Keys
Black Betsy Keys
Bob Keys
Shell Keys

Buttonwood Keys
Club Key
Russell Key
Manatee Keys

FLORIDA BAY

Since its discovery the Everglades has captured the imagination of all who have ventured here. The subtropical environment is unique in all of North America. Geologists come here to study the park because it is a land in the making. This flat watery expanse is a haven for birds which find their foodsource in its shallow waters. A matter of inches in water level can mean a difference in habitats. Long intrigued by the park's biological variety, such as the many orchids, trees, 52 color forms of Liguus snails, reptiles, mammals, and plants, the professional scientist and casual visitor alike have been fascinated by this subtropical paradise. Its subtle diversity must be studied closely and slowly. The rewards of an Everglades visit are many. As the story continues, how well we manage it will be told by future generations.

CARR CLIFTON

This tranquil scene of Florida Bay does not reflect the many storms this lone tree has weathered.

FRED HIRSCHMANN

⚠ *A tropical band of mangroves wraps around the world with a tenacious grip. Beneficial for food, shelter, and nesting sites for wildlife, they are also land builders. However, international development and reclamation projects have reduced mangrove forests to a fraction of what they once were. Everglades National Park is a model to inspire a global effort in the preservation of this valuable prolific habitat.*

Inside back cover: *Water, sky,* ▷ *and land have interacted since time immemorial to form the Everglades. Photo by Connie Toops.*

Back cover: *An alligator surveys* ▷ *his domain while sunning. Photo by Glenn Van Nimwegen.*

Books in this "*in pictures ... The Continuing Story*" series are: Arches & Canyonlands, Bryce Canyon, Crater Lake, Death Valley, Everglades, Glacier, Glen Canyon-Lake Powell, Grand Canyon, Grand Teton, Hawai`i Volcanoes, Mount Rainier, Mount St. Helens, Olympic, Petrified Forest, Rocky Mountain, Sequoia & Kings Canyon, Yellowstone, Yosemite, Zion.

Translation Packages are also available. Each title can be ordered with a booklet in German, French, or Japanese bound into the center of the English book. Selected titles in both this series and our other books are available in up to 8 languages.

The original National Park series, "The Story Behind the Scenery," covers over 75 parks and related areas. Other series include one on **Indian culture,** and the **"Voyage of Discovery"** series on the expansion of the western United States. To receive our catalog with over 110 titles:

Call (800-626-9673), fax (702-433-3420), or write to the address below.

Published by KC Publications, 3245 E. Patrick Ln., Suite A, Las Vegas, NV 89120.

Created, Designed, and Published in the U.S.A.
Printed by Doosan Dong-A Co., Ltd., Seoul, Korea
Paper produced exclusively by Hankuk Paper Mfg. Co., Ltd.